Read Me
At Your
Own Risk

Jeffrey L. Kubiak

To Nicole
my classmate and Friend

Jeffrey Kubiak

Tech High '89

Note for Librarians: a cataloguing record for this book that includes Dewey Classification and US Library of Congress numbers is available from the National Library of Canada. The complete cataloguing record can be obtained from the National Library's online database at: www.nlc-bnc.ca/amicus/index-e.html

ISBN 1-4122-0000-8

TRAFFORD

This book was published *on-demand* in cooperation with Trafford Publishing.
On-demand publishing is a unique process and service of making a book available for retail sale to the public taking advantage of on-demand manufacturing and Internet marketing.
On-demand publishing includes promotions, retail sales, manufacturing, order fulfilment, accounting and collecting royalties on behalf of the author.

Suite 6E, 2333 Government St., Victoria, B.C. V8T 4P4, CANADA

Phone	250-383-6864	Toll-free	1-888-232-4444 (Canada & US)
Fax	250-383-6804	E-mail	sales@trafford.com
Web site	www.trafford.com	TRAFFORD PUBLISHING IS A DIVISION OF TRAFFORD HOLDINGS LTD.	
Trafford Catalogue #03-1636		www.trafford.com/robots/03-1636.html	

10   9   8   7   6   5   4   3   2

This book is dedicated to my four children Christian, Jared, Joshua and Caitlin.

A special thanks to my guest poets Claire Strough, Anne Marie McMahon & Jennifer L. Olague Balkus for donating their work to this project. A special thanks to the staff at Trafford Publishing, Inc. for making this book possible.

About the Author

I am a resident of Buffalo, New York and am the proud father of four wonderful (most of the time) children. I started writing poetry more or less as a joke but my writing took an unusual turn and become more serious. My friends surprised by my work are the ones who lit the fire under my feet to try and publish my work. For better or worse this book is the result.

Contact the author
Website: www.JeffreyLKubiak.com
E-Mail: JeffreyLKubiak@aol.com
USPS :   P.O. Box 478
              Buffalo, NY 14207

Table of Contents

Guest Poets

Read Me at Your Own Risk

What shall I write next?
Not much just TEXT
Quite basic is my prose
My lack of talent shows
But hey, I don't care
Hey!! Look over there!
Ha ha made your head turn
And more space I burn
In life I'm no poet
And yes I know it
This poem makes no sense
At least I ain't tense
Some people think I'm quite off
Well, I laugh as they scoff
At least I live life and be happy
And yes at times I'm sappy
Sometimes I seem rude
And often quite crude
So if my words bother you one bit
Go roll in a pile of $h!*
I write what I write
Never mean to spite
I talk silly for fun
Mean ill to none
So remember you've been warned
And don't let it be ignored
READ ME AT YOUR OWN RISK!!

Those Three Words

I hear you say those three words
So tender and so sweet
My heart beckons back
My mind stops it in its tracks
I've been wounded deep
My heart is just too weak
These wounds are healing slowly
As we grow closer day by day
With you, everything I want to share
You're nursing my broken heart
Helping it recover
From the damage of another
But my mind is still afraid
To protect my wounded heart
It blocks the message
Upon my lips it freezes the words
I know you long to hear
Those three special words
I'm sorry, but just for now
It's just to hard to say

A Walk in the Fields

I'm having a drink
I need time to think
I head for that field o'er yonder
I have many things to ponder
For in reality I have been caught
Now I need time for much thought

So I head for the tall grass
Watching the clouds pass
I'm thinking of my life
And all of my strife
Which way should I turn
To find what I must learn

I look down at my feet
I see lies and deceit
I look around and see
My troubles devour me
I look to the clouds above
And I see it…. God's love

Without You

What would I do without you?
Where would life's journey take me?
When you died it was a tragedy
Without you......I have no clue

You were an angel born into my life
From the time our eyes first met
I knew I owed God a great debt
Without you...My life is full of strife

A bat of your lashes, a silly face
Your smile could make me melt
My deepest feelings you have felt
Without you...A hole I can't replace

You were a baby, only three
You would bounce and play on my lap
You would sing and you would clap
Without you...I have an empty knee

People die and now your gone
Why God took you I can't be sure
Maybe your soul was just too pure
Without you......I must live on

Lost in the Past

The sun has dawned on a new day
It begins to boil the morning fog away
Yet my mind remains in its own haze
It still dwells upon my yesterdays

The sun has brought the day anew
But my mind is still in review
Of the choices I made at another time
I dwell in the past as the church bells chime

My mind is torn asunder
As through the past I blunder
I'm stuck in a past that will eat & devour
While the present slips by hour after hour

I'm pondering choices I already made
Within my swirling thoughts I wade
On the sea of broken dreams, I am lost
My present and future, the cost

The Whittler

To my eyes it's nothing more than a block of wood
To the whittler, a horse, maybe it could
With tools as simple as an old pocket knife
He could carve a statue for his wife
He sees each block as potential art
He eyes it down, unsure where to start
He eyes it deeply, he sees right into it's core
It's inner beauty, he wants to explore
He stares with much intent
Pondering for what this block is meant
He begins to carve with his rugged hands
He whittles, shaves and sands
He works his magic for hours and hours
Extracting the blocks inner power
His hands whittle with untold grace
He dabs the sweat from his face
He works until his blade is worn
For his daughter, a new unicorn

Life Without A Net

You fly through the air with the greatest of ease
For the cheering crowd, you aim to please
You fly through the air from swing to swing
You live for the rush, this is your thing
You trust your partner to keep you from harm
Spinning, twirling, flipping into their arms
Just praying your timing is right
Living your life in the spotlight
Ooo's and ahhs are what you hear
As the air rushes through your hair
You challenge gravity just for fun
You love the applause when the show is done
Your shows a hit, your timing is right
You smile, you bow and slip out of sight
You take a breathe and wipe your sweat
This is life without a net

Why?

I'm tired, nodding off to sleep
My thoughts are wrapped around you
I can't hold you now, I'm feeling blue
Memories of you I keep

Sleep grabs me in its icy grip
Drags me deep into my own mind
My deepest thoughts are what I find
Sending me on an unthinkable trip

I see a blurred vision off in the distance
I clear my mind for a better view
I see a beautiful vision of you
I long for you this very instance

You look perfect, like an angel
You float upon white graceful wings
There's beautiful music as an angel sings
The angel lifts you, your body dangles

That's when I realize, you are dead
I release my anger unto you
You can't leave, we have much to do
Who's going to tuck me into bed?

I chase the angel as it lifts you to the sky
I try to get one last kiss
The angel rises, I miss
I scream at God, I just ask why?

Why can't I at least say good-bye?
Mom I love you with all my heart
In heaven I know you'll do your part
But who will hold me when I cry?

Tears flow freely down my face
The angel smiles and gives me a wink
Dear child you'll understand, just think
Dear child your tears are no disgrace

Years have now passed by
I can still feel that you care
But the pain is still there
God, I still don't understand why?

An angel appeared in my sleep last night
Dear child you really need to ponder why
There is no need to say good-bye
She's still here, she's just out of sight

Where Have You Gone Dr. Seuss?

I've loved storybooks since I was a child
Dr. Seuss was my favorite, he was wild
But where have you gone dear Dr. Seuss
I miss your rhymes like a sticklenoose
Remember the wocket in your pocket
I laughed my eye right out of its socket
And of course that crazy Cat in the Hat
For him, I'd roll out the welcome mat
Who else could make you eat green eggs and ham
Heck, that's how my mom got me to eat Spam
I used to like Hop on Pop
Until my kids hopped on pop
You made us think the things we can think
I just thought a purple snortle in my sink
Your rhymes may never have made much sense
It didn't stop the whatzit from hopping the fence
I loved your stories nonsensical and wild
I wish nothing more than to share them with my child
So dear Dr. Seuss and your wild zoo
Now that I'm grown, I can say THANK YOU

Like Robert Frost

Like Robert Frost
Two paths I crossed
The fork in the middle
Has posed me a riddle
The choice once again was posed
Shall I choose the less traveled road?
Or the beaten path should I choose?
I sit, think and take a quick snooze
I dream of the choice before me
An answer I hope to foresee
I awake confused and dazed
The answer came and I was amazed
I decided to blaze my own trail
I chose to write my own tale

The Unknown Letter

This letter is sealed with a kiss
I want you to know it's you I miss
I'm sorry I had to go away
I hoped to see you again someday
I said I love you and walked out the door
For my country has sent me off to war
To you, I will not lie
I am afraid to die
I did not start this battle
I'd rather be home raising cattle
I'm not sure if you will get this letter
This battle could be going better
A lot of soldiers lie here dead
I have blood dripping from my head
Our supplies are running short
Communications down, can't report
There are no signs of relief
Friends all dead, racked with grief
The enemy is approaching fast
My time has come at last
I cower in my foxhole in fear
No ammo, my death is near
For my country, I will stand
I will die with bayonet in hand
Grenades and bullets I may lack
I won't die with a hole in my back

Does She Know?

Does she know I still care?
Did I tell her?
Did I dare?
Did I tell her how I loved her eyes?
Does she know or even realize?
Does she know I love her hair
and how I love the time we share?
Does she know I think she's funny
or how when she's around it's always sunny?
Did I dare?
Did I share?
Did I tell her how I cared?
Alas, I didn't.
She died last night in her sleep.
The Lord took her soul to keep.
She left without knowing
because my feelings weren't showing.
So,
If there's feelings there,
Please dare,
Please share,
Please tell her that you care.

The Mistake

I made a mistake
My lies, I cannot fake
I felt so weak
The affair, I didn't seek
My heart is with you
Yet I have made you blue
Your feelings, I never meant to harm
Why didn't I resist her charm ?
Please let me at least explain
I will not try to shift blame
I've been having a rough time at work
You see, this client is a real jerk
So my boss, she's been working me late
Trust me, it was never a date
We had an important contract due
If we didn't finish, he would sue
We both felt under a lot of stress
It's no fun working under duress
We worked all week to finish the deal
We toiled long and finished it with zeal

We pitched the contract over dinner
Our client thought it was a winner
On the dotted line he did sign
Over a bottle of very fine wine
We had a few victory drinks
We didn't even really think
We were excited over our deal
Another big client we did seal
We returned to the office to file the contract
That is where we made first contact
She brushed up against me with her breast
I shied away, I knew that was what's best
She smiled and blushed red
Next thing I know we're in bed
What we did it was a sin
How could I ever let it begin ?
I know I can't ask you to forgive
Because with this guilt I must live
So I will live riddled with my guilt
For I have destroyed what love had built

The Mighty Arrow

One day there was an untold battle
Fought with bows and arrows
Long before pale man walked the land
Over a magic arrow they fought
The battle raged for days before all was lost
Until the owner of the arrow
Unleashed it in desperation
The mighty arrow
Ended that fight
Only the arrow survived to tell the tale

Many years later the arrow was found
Found by a boy on the old battlefield
Where long ago it ended the untold battle
The boys father was quite mean
His boy showed him the arrow anyways
His father got mad and took the arrow
He tried to snap it right in half
The mighty arrow
Ended that fight
Only it survived to tell the tale

One day I wandered into an old cabin
I found the ancient arrow lying there
When I touched it, its story it told
It's name was Peacemaker
I held its power, I understood
In an act of desperation, I bury the arrow
For my whole world is at war
The mighty arrow
Ended that fight
Only it survived to tell the tale

Once again Peacemaker ruled
Humanity gone, it'll rest for a while
Until evolution brings another race
To defile and desecrate a beautiful world
One day it will again wield its power
It will awake from its slumber
And make peace rule again
The mighty arrow
Will end that fight
Only it will survive to tell the tale

I Should Have Listened

I asked my mom for advice.
With her, I did not agree.
Mom would have a fit
if she knew what I just did.
She told me not to do it.
Of course I didn't listen.
I ignored her advice.
Why didn't she tell me she was right?
Now I have a big regret.
Dad will flip too I bet.
Sooner or later I must face them.
What will they say?
What will they do?
I should have listened.
Oh my! What a mess!
Now I am so embarrassed.
How long will this last?
How will I explain
that I now have a purple Mohawk?

My Friend Fred

Hello to my friend Fred
I like to hit him on the head
With a loaf of stale bread
Or an old tire with no tread
Our friendship is tried and true
So I beat him black and blue
Dip his foot in super glue
And make him wear a bowling shoe
I beat him with an old mail post
Like some bad TV host
In his face I rub hot buttered toast
Yet he plays with me the most
Yes boys will be boys
We fight over girls and toys
In spite of all of this anger
He's never a stranger

Why?????

Because Fred is my friend

Dear Sweetheart

Dear Sweetheart,
For now we are apart
This is just a simple note
To show its you, whom I dote
I treasure the time we spend together
No matter the time or weather
With you, I stand tall like a sailboat's mast
But our time together passes much too fast
I long for your arms wrapped in a hug
Apart, time slips slowly like a slug
I know I will see you tomorrow
But until then, my hearts in sorrow
I miss you so dearly, I can't finish my meal
It's important that you know how I feel
I long for your lips wrapped in a kiss
Because it's you alone that I miss
I can't wait to feel your touch
Sweetheart, I miss you so much

Dear Mommy

Dear Mommy,
You don't know me yet
But you will soon, I bet
So let me introduce myself
I'm a gift from God's great wealth
I'm your baby sent from God above
I'm sent here with an angels love
My soul is pure
Of that I am sure
I will love you heart and soul
Without a fee, without a toll
God made me from your passion
He molded me in his own fashion
In return I won't ask for much
I need your tender and loving touch
I need your arms to hold me to your chest
I need your milk from your breast
I need you to teach me and to guide
I need your promise before I come outside

With God's love,
Your Child

Wasted Space

I just read a poem
about a guy
He isn't very shy
Yes you know him

He types dumb rhymes
That make so little sense
His brain is quite dense
He likes to waste your time

It should be unlawful
For him to be so rude
He's really quite crude
His poetry is awful

He is a disgrace
To writers abroad
If near me he trod
I'd smack his face

He mocks in your face
His words are a waste
He has really bad taste
He just wasted our space

Lost in the Sixties

Though I am now in my fifties
My mind is lost in the sixties
Upon my mind a picture I draw
All those women burning bras
Those were the good old days
When the sky was a purple haze
I made love not war
Our voice they couldn't ignore
I was rebellious and free
Watched Woodstock naked in a tree
Saw Hendrix, The Doors and The Dead
Watched them all with thunder overhead
Tumultuous times these were
To me they were mostly a blur
Lost in a cloud of smoke
It was the seventies when I awoke
Somehow disco had taken a grip
Or was this just another bad trip

The Dark Secret

A big dark secret I did learn
But you see I'm not brave
I'm taking it to my grave
On my mind this secret does burn

I learned it with my black magic
I practice the dark art
With my secret I must depart
My secret is far to tragic

Human life is overpriced
The soul holds much more power
As I near this final hour
I now know that I'm the anti-Christ

I've done no evil since my birth
Told my fate by the dark angels
The world in my hands now dangles
I love humanity for what its worth

My lot in life has been cast
I have been left with no choice
Prodded by this evil voice
Satan will walk the world at last

You see, my secret is quite serious
Upon this power that evil brings
The whole world now clings
It's making my mind delirious

I never knew this future loomed
I thought as a person I was decent
But these changes in me, so recent
Because of me the world is doomed

Ordered to perform mass homicide
The future doesn't look so bright
I really must do what is right
I write this note before my suicide

You must understand why my life, I gave
I'm sorry mom but I really must go
I just had to make sure that you know
I'm going to hell but the world I did save

The Whirling Vortex

I hang my head with much despair
Another gloomy autumn is here
It's sad and gloomy, it makes me cry
The trees seem weak as their leaves dry

A gentle fall breeze blows down my street
It's blowing dried leaves around my feet
The bright autumn leaves they fall, they die
The weeping willows, they seem to cry

The breeze is now a strong autumn gust
It takes the remaining leaves into its trust
The leaves come rolling down my street
More and more swirl around my feet

The gust is now swirling all around me
The leaves start dancing for me to see
They spin and dance in a swirling motion
Soon I think I get their notion

I close my eyes and raise my arms to the sky
Within the swirling winds I hear a sigh
The whirling vortex wraps me in a blanket of leaves
It's power stuns me, It's so hard to believe

Within the vortex I am now carried
Covered in leaves, I feel buried
The vortex speaks in natures tongues
It sucks the air right from my lungs

The vortex carries me up into the clouds
The leaves follow with their rustling sounds
The city below is vibrant and wired
While the barren trees sag and look tired

The vortex shows me that this is what's best
The trees are so tired and now they must rest
The vortex shows me that I need not be sad
When they bloom again next spring, I'll be glad

The vortex now sets me unto the ground
The leaves land with their rustling sound
I put down my arms and open my eyes
I look around and I hear nature's sigh

The vortex has shown me the trees are just weary
And I shouldn't think of autumn as dark & dreary
Gloomy skies & barren trees may give me a creep
But now I know that they only need sleep

Thanks to the vortex I have seen the light
Autumn is just the trees saying goodnight
So now I see autumn as natures rest
In spring they'll be back with zest

Walking on Cloud Nine

I'm walking on cloud nine
Up where the sun shines
Life has taken a new angle
I swear, I'm touched by an angel
Life is no longer bad
I'm through being sad
The little things no longer bother me
My happiness is plain to see
Life has tossed a gift in my lap
Mending my heart, filling the gap
I'm flying on the wings of a dove
Because I have found a new love
So now I'm doing just fine
I'm walking on cloud nine

Sending My Heart

I see a beautiful vision, it's you
I fell for you, I had no clue
I don't mean to dramatize
I did really just realize
You're everything I've sought for
Plus your so much more
To let you go would be a mistake
It'd be my loss, my heartbreak
So I'll hang on real tight
Hug you with all my might
I'll stay right by your side
No matter how rough the ride
My feelings towards you are true
That's why, I'm sending my heart out to you

Fueled By Coffee

I awake tired and groggy
My mind jumbled and foggy
I need my morning fix
I know just what to mix
I have a craving to feed
I know just what I need
Caffeine will give me a jolt
So off to work I can bolt
Before I can leave my abode
I grab another mug for the road
Off to work people skitter
I'm getting my first jitter
I pull into my parking space
Wipe some coffee from my face
I walk in with an empty mug
Fill it fast and down I chug
Now my hands begin to shake
Drank too much, my mistake
But my day would be choppy
If I wasn't fueled by coffee

Writers Block

My mind drawing a blank
Frustration, I cannot fake
No thoughts come to mind
Tense, I need to unwind
Oh! For the love of Pete!
Deadline, I must meet
I have writers block indeed
Inspiration, a new idea I need
In dire need of another verse
Ideas, in my mind I rehearse
Chewing on the end of my pen
Stressed, I erase my words again
Against my desk I slam my book
Angry, my desk shook
Where have my words gone?
Confused, I pace the front lawn
Brain locked down, no words to find
Sleeping, to clear my mind
Lost in my own desperation
Begging, I need inspiration
Sitting staring at the clock
Panicked, This is writers block

Hey Bartender

Hey bartender
Pass me a drink
I don't want to think
I've worked all day and now I'm tired
I need a stiff drink to get me wired
I need to relieve my stress
Check out that girl in the tight dress

Hey bartender
Pass me another one
I'm getting loose and having fun
Time for me to get wild
Maybe act like a child
Hey maybe I'll flirt
With the girl in the short skirt

Hey bartender
I need another round
I can still see the ground
The music is loud
Now there's quite a crowd
I think I'll make a pass
At the girl with the nice ass

Hey bartender
Can I buy you a drink?
My self control is on the brink
So what's your sign?
You're look really fine
I think your hot
Please let me buy you a shot

Hey bartender
I need more alcohol
I think I'm going to fall
The bar is in a tizzy
And I'm feeling dizzy
I have to get this off my chest
Can I grab your breast?

Hey bartender
Why did you spray mace in my eye?
Who is this big mean guy?
Why is he grabbing me by my shirt?
Why did he just throw me in the dirt?
Why is my eye turning black and blue?
Hey!! Fine !! No tip for you!!!

Our Camping Trip

Summer is finally here
Grab your camping gear
Time for a weekend at the state park
We must pitch camp before dark
Travel for hours along the highway
We sing a song to pass time away
Finally our destination, we reach
This is no picnic at the beach
Unpack the car and pitch the tent
Time to use the gear we rent
Dad starts a roaring campfire
While we go play in the muck and mire
Walking trails and climbing rocks
Mom's busy unpacking our extra socks
Time to cook hot dogs on a stick
While at the mosquitoes we flick
It's peaceful here, quiet and mellow
Time for us to toast marshmallows
Off to sleep in our sleeping bags
Time for ghost stories and gags
We got scared by a hooting owl
I think we heard a bear growl
Then came the rain drip, drip, drip
What a way to end our camping trip

A Natural Day

The green grass grows in the morning sun
The morning dew still clinging to every blade
The flowers begin to open down in the glade
The birds are singing for everyone

The sun peaks up over the first hill
The rabbits and foxes run through the fields
They wake to the power that nature wields
They eat from the land, but only take their fill

The sun rolls across the pond
Out come the turtles to sun their shells
On the log which under they dwell
They eat small fish of which they are fond

The sun has now risen and brought nature to life
The animals hunt and search for their food
Their methods are quite basic and crude
They live a life full of struggle and strife

The struggle of nature is quite a sight
We see creatures frolic and play
Little do we know they have no time to play
For soon will come the creatures of the night

The sun now setting, brings the day to an end
The rabbits and foxes return to their dens
The turtles return to the ponds and the fens
For now they become hunted and need to defend

What is the Sense?

What is the sense?
It's a question so immense.
Where are we going
without even knowing?
How will we get there
if we don't know where?
Why do we follow
into the empty hollow?
Why do we pray
when we hear no voice say
if we are right
and we put up a good fight
or if we are wrong
and don't belong?
Why do we believe
when people die and grieve?

Well... We just do

Self Realization

What gives me the right to get out of bed
and already have this notion in my head?
How can I know that today
is going to be another bad day?
What gives me the right to be so negative?
Am I really that insensitive?
Each day should begin with a new slate.
I can't live in this miserable state.
I need to be more positive.
A little more sensitive.
Each day is its own page.
So get passed this depressed stage.
Force myself to smile.
It'll become real after a while.
Hold my chin up high.
Let my worries go in a big sigh.
Take a breath and hold it deep.
Exhale the old, you don't need to keep.
Live today as a new day.
Live happy, live your way.

Myth of the Fairytale Ending

Once upon a time
I heard wedding bells chime
My own fairytale had begun
Soon came the end of the fun
Together we thought we were perfect
But our differences we did soon detect
Our life paths diverged
Our future no longer merged
We split and wandered our own way
Both searching for a better day
You see,
Once upon a time does not always end
With they lived happily ever after

A Walk Along the Ocean Shore

Sometimes I long to be alone
I don't want all my feelings shown
So I head for the ocean shore
To ponder what life has in store
Over the ocean the sun has now dawned
Along the shore my footprints are drawn
This is the peace and serenity I wish
As I watch the gulls diving for fish
I stare blankly as the waters crash the shore
My mind wanders as I think some more
I stroll down toward the boat dock
The rest of the world, I now block
I remove my sandals and take a seat
I wait for the next wave to soak my feet
I'm thinking about things I deplore
As the next wave crashes into the shore
The water washes my thoughts away
My mind cleansed clean, I begin to sway
I'm waiting for the Lord, My soul to teach
As I ramble down that long lonely beach
I have lost my life's inspiration
And now I seek it in desperation

Ode to the Mailman

The sun beating down
Hot, humid, summers dog days
Boiling, sticky summer haze
Hot and sweaty, I frown

Baking, frying under the sun
The mailman delivers the mail
Delivers it without fail
Working in the blistering heat isn't fun

The rain comes beating down
Lightning crashes, thunder rumbles
Winds pick up, a garbage can tumbles
Cold and wet, I frown

Shoes sopping, soaking wet
The mailman delivers the mail
Delivers it without fail
Do I hate the rain? You bet!

The snow comes beating down
The temperature dips
Frozen, broken, chapped lips
Numb and wet, I frown

Trudging through heavy winter snows
The mailman delivers the mail
Delivers it without fail
Yes, working in the snow really blows

The mailman beaten down
Large boxes, fat catalogs
Alone on the street, little dialog
Sore and tire, I frown

He rings your bell once in awhile
The mailman delivers the mail
Delivers it without fail
Gives you that box with a smile

I'm Bored

Today I'm just bored
I feel so ignored
My nickname is Crazy
And I'm kind of lazy
I hate doing dishes
I hate scaling fishes
This poem will make no sense
And make me look dense
But I have to pass time away
So I will do it my way
My honey has been in the shower
For better than an hour
I don't really care
Because I'll soon be there
So I sit here and rhyme
As I try to pass time
My mind is lost in a haze
But my honey doesn't faze
So with my friend I will fight
And beat with all my might
We'll fight till its not funny
For the laughs of my honey
So I'll just ramble on
As another TV show comes on

I wander out my door
Maybe head for the store
As I was pushing my shopping cart
I heard someone rip a loud fart
Oooh boy who was that geek
Because boy oh boy did that reek
I'm sorry I had to laugh
At the old ladies gaff
I lifted my finger to point
She hurried out of the joint
It was worth the look on her face
The look of shock and disgrace
But hey do you think I really care
I even laughed at her blue hair
So why did I even go to the store
I don't know, maybe to ramble some more
So does any of this make sense?
Can I really be this dense?
Nope ! I'm really quite well
Just hanging in my padded cell
So what's the moral of this story
Don't write poetry for glory
So if by this you are floored
I'm sorry ....I'm bored

Old and Gray

I'm old and gray
I've had my better days
Age crept up on me
It's plain for all to see

My wrinkles,
Are signs of my wisdom
My sagging cheeks,
Show the pain I've seen
My eyes,
Show I'm tired and weary
My smile,
Shows I'm young at heart

I may be old and gray
And seen so many days
But my wisdom you cannot measure
Because I am a golden treasure

Am I Crazy?

I sit here staring blankly in my padded cell
My family put me here, they thought I wasn't well
My mind swayed and swirled
I drifted off to my own world
Much more perfect than our own
Endless fields of flowers have grown
Vibrant & brilliant colors abound
A rainbow laid upon the ground
Maybe this sounds kind of sappy
But this world is always happy
There are no wars, there is no strife
All of us here live a long and happy life
We never want for food or drink
It's peaceful and lets us think
Here there is no pain or anger
You need not fear, there is no danger
My earthly body may sit and stare
But my soul moves freely here
So is my mind really hazy?
Do you think I'm really crazy?
I'm doing quite well staring in my padded cell
While you live in a world that has gone to hell
I'll live in my world of delusions
You can keep your world of illusions

Send Me An Angel

I am so cold and all alone
I lost my job and my home
I must now live on the street
Beg from the people I meet
My clothes are now old & worn
Even my last sock is torn
From the garbage I ate my last meal
I pretended it was potatoes and veal
I feel like I want to jump in a lake
But what I really need is a break
I don't want to live like a louse
I want to live in my own house
So I ask God "What's your angle?"
"Please send me an angel"

The Wedding Oath

On this, our wedding day
There's so much left to say
These words I choose to say now
As we take our wedding vow
We exchange our feelings from within
For today our future together begins
We now begin the rest of our life
There will be struggle and strife
Together our problems, we'll solve
Each trial will help us evolve
A relationship is built upon trust
Have faith in each other, we must
Hand in hand, each trial we'll meet
As one, each trial we will defeat
There will be no I or me
From now on its us or we
With you, everything I'll share
Because its you, for whom I care
Today, as we share this point of view
All that's left to say is "I Love You"

Living for the Dollar

It's a mad dash
A race for the cash
Join the rat race
And all of its disgrace
Fueled by our greed
We leave others in need
For others I don't care
Take mine if you dare
Get a new sports car
To top your neighbors new bar
Driven by vanity
Into insanity
Yes, in God we may trust
But worship the dollar we must
It's enough to make you holler
When you're living for the dollar

Lost Utopia

Imagine a world
without a computer,
a video game,
a TV, radio or car.
No movies, no pool halls,
gas or electricity.
No malls or shopping centers.
Can you imagine?
How would we live
without these simple
necessities of life?
Imagine a peaceful garden
filled with flowers and trees.
A beautiful rainbow
spread out before you.
The quiet, the serenity,
the peace and the innocence.
We had it all.
Look how we blew it.
We took perfection
and we tried to improve it.
Yet all we accomplished
was a lost utopia.

Through Evil's Eyes

Crouching, creeping,
in the shadows.
Wild thoughts,
an evil voice,
it urges me onward.
I must taste her
precious blood.
So pretty,
so young,
an unsuspecting innocent.
A glint of cold steel
reflects in the moonlight.
I lie just out of sight.
Come closer dear.
I lunge.
I grab.
I drag her to the brush.
Her eyes are wide with terror
I can smell her fear.
I smile with glee.
I tease her with my knife.
Her sweet hot blood
splatters my face.
This is my ecstasy.

Route Six Sixty Six

Blood runs red
On the highway of the dead
The rain washes it into the ditch
It doesn't care, poor or rich
Worse than dead man's curve
Your dead before the last swerve
This is the highway to hell
Upon it, Satan has cast his spell
Doomed to eternal pain
Your cries are in vain
Falling through a bottomless hole
Demons gnawing on your soul
Satan grabs you in his deadly grip
This is the end of your road trip
So be careful where you turn
Or in hell you will burn
It's too late for your crucifix
Once you turn down route six sixty six

Can You Help Me Love Again?

Once again my heart is broken
Love seems so base and token
Betrayed once more
Knocked to the floor
Heart torn asunder
through life I blunder
Destroyed, I cannot trust
My heart refuses to adjust
It's tired of taking damage
It's put my love in storage
I'm tired of love knocking me to the ground
I'm not sure I can handle another round
This time I'm staying down
I don't want to wear loves crown
My wounds are more than skin deep
It's made love seem so cheap
I'm beaten, broken and confused
I feel as if I've been abused
My heart continues to bleed
Strength is what I need
Can you help me love again?

Savior of my Heart

Your love has set me free
My past can now let me be
You reach deeply into my heart
Urging me to make a fresh start
You inspire me to write like a bard
You wait for me to drop my guard
My mind has built a great wall
You attack with your love, pieces fall
You are determined not to fail
If you stop, your heart will wail
Slowly chipping away at my defense
I break and crumble, the pain is intense
Unchained, I cry and weep
My despair I can no longer keep
I let it out in a loud scream
Your arms hold my new dream
This opening is long overdue
I'm now free and for that I love you
You have given me a fresh start
You are the savior of my heart

Celestial Light Show

One starry night
a comet streaked by,
lighting up the night sky.
Trailing its unknown vapors,
leaving a sparkling trail.
It was a celestial light show.
Its beauty was unsurpassed.
This icy ball was immense.
Hurling towards the earth
which had no defense.
Each night the comet drew closer.
Pretty soon the earth would know
that it was going to be a part
of the celestial light show.

The Bitter End

I am lost and confused
Left feeling used
You said that you loved me
Your lies I couldn't see
I was held in loves handcuffs
Your words were just a bluff
I was blinded by emotion
Set adrift on the lovers ocean
We were together so long
Where did I go wrong?
I was always there for you
About your affair I had no clue
I was naïve and refused to believe
The truth seeped through a sieve
As your lies spread like tines on a fork
Your spell unraveled and failed to work
I now see through all of your lies
It's you I now hate and despise
You tried to cover your tracks
Consistency is what your story lacks
Your tongue now tied in knots
Our love festers and rots
Like an oozing, infected sore
It rots right to the core
I gave you my heart and soul
You ground it up in an old mixing bowl
So to you this message I send
This is it .... the bitter end

I Get By

I have no fortune
That I can mention
Though I'm not poor
Like most, I can use more
But I get by…
I work and toil
Under the sun I boil
I work all day
I must earn my pay
But I get by…
My job it ain't great
But it pays for my date
A mansion my house is not
But I'm thankful for the one I got
But I get by…
I thought I met my true love
The one sent from above
Our lives began with our children
But ended in a black cauldron
But I get by…
My future looks hazy and gray
But I dream of a better day
It starts with a white dove
It's leading me towards a new love
And I get by…

The Vagrant

Today I met a vagrant on the street.
Not the kind of guy you'd like to meet.
He was dirty and had a bad smell,
but many words of wisdom he did tell.
He said sometimes you win others you fail.
Either way it is your life's tale.
Always trust and follow your heart.
Do it right from the start.
Never be ashamed when you lose.
At least you used your will to choose.
Be proud but humble when you win.
Don't let your ego swell, conceit is a sin.
For those who helped you along the way,
thank you is what you need to say.
Also thank those who were against you.
To them your determination is due.
Everyone you meet plays a role in your life.
From me, the vagrant to your dear wife.
I replied, "I don't mean to criticize.
Why are you a vagrant if you're so wise?"
He replied, "You are my success tale.
I made humanity. Please do not fail."
He smiled and vanished into the thin air.
I followed his advice, that's why I'm writing here.

The Sketch

I like to sit and doodle.
Today I sketch a poodle.
It is playing catch
with a boy, a perfect match.
The yard is fenced in.
A passing truck raises a din.
Overhead a bird flies free.
The yard has a big oak tree,
a swing made from a tire and rope.
A small boy will sit and mope.
Swinging is a bigger boy
teasing him, holding his toy.
We can't ignore the little girl
making her toy baton twirl.
Add colors to complete
kids playing in the summer heat.

Anatomy of A Poem

Staring at a blank page
Wondering what words will fill it
Waiting for inspiration to hit
The page is my stage

Upon it I place my text
At first a stray verse or line
That will tie together in time
Not knowing what I'll write next

No preconceived topic on hand
I write as words come to mind
Not knowing how it'll unwind
Scribbling at my minds command

Writing in the moment
Madly when on a roll
On my mind, it takes a toll
If no words come, I torment

Relaxed in the tub, it's a word fest
My mind shuts down under duress
I don't write well under stress
Quiet and peaceful, I'm at my best

Country Morning

The moon
Pal and fading
The sun
Seething and rising
The lake
Calm and placid
The wind
Gentle and refreshing
The trees
Steadfast and swaying
The birds
Musical and graceful
The fog
Murky and mysterious
The rabbits
Playful and timid
The fox
Stealthy and sly
The horse
Strong and valiant
The deer
Curious and shy
Me
Amazed and awed
By the beauty of the country morning

Me

Stressed,
tense, jumpy,
quiet, distracted,
In need of escape.
Disgruntled,
mean, ornery,
crabby, angry,
get out of my way.
Depressed,
sad, moody,
blue, lonely,
I need a hug from you.
Confused,
misdirected, lost,
unsure, undecided,
I need your guidance.
Happy,
smiling, joyful,
joking, frivolous,
lots of fun to be with.
Me,
stressed, disgruntled,
depressed, confused
happy, loving.
This is how it feels to be me.

Washed Away

Laying back in my steaming tub
Soothing heat, eases my tension
Washes away my stress

Soothing bubbles cover me up
Popping bubbles, cleansing my pores
Washes away today's grime

Rising steam jades the room from view
It's my reprieve from the real world
Washes away my reality

Hot cloth covers my face
Eyes roll back, my mind now free
Washes away my cares

Fighting kids outside my door
A smash, a crash, a scream
Washes away my serenity

How Crazy Got His Padded Cell

Today I'm visiting my shrink
He thinks it's irrational how I think
As usual I'm bored
Am I being ignored?
I hope not
I'm staring at an ink blot
My doctor asks me what I see
I see his wife down on her knee
She's polishing my shoe
They are suede, they are blue
He asked me why I thought that
I said "I just wanted to chat."
So he gave me some Prozac pills
With one hundred refills
Wow, he must think I'm crazy
Just because my judgment is hazy
He said that I am not normal
I told him he dresses way to formal
So he gives me a new jacket
All those belts and buckles make a racket
He rings a little silver bell
Two big men drag me to my padded cell
Now I can safely bounce and play
Sit back and live life my way

Dog Days

Sweat dripping from my face
Seeping out of my pores
I'm heated to the core
My body is a sticky, sweaty disgrace

My flesh sticks to my seat
This is the worst that I have felt
Even the blacktop has begun to melt
I've got to beat this summer heat

It must be a hundred in the shade
Under attack by the solar tyrant
Break open a fire hydrant
In the water, for hours we wade

Hot and humid, this is a bummer
Much to warm for having fun
Hide in the shade and curse the sun
These are the dog days of summer

Comatose

I lie here waiting for death to claim me
Just staring blankly at the ceiling
I cannot move, I have no feeling
The ceiling above me is all I see

I'm still here, my mind still thinks
My body is no longer mine to use
They won't let me die, they refuse
I'm going insane, I'm on the brink

Time is confused and muddled, reality lost
My mind is tired, I do not sleep
The plug they won't pull, they want to keep
Let me die, save yourself the cost

Make the choice, why do you hesitate?
Let me go, are you clueless?
My earthly body is useless
Do you think I'm here to meditate?

Why do you continue to torture me?
I'm only a shell, have you no guilt?
Alive because of this machine they built
My body is already dead, cant you see?

That one last moment my mind is clear
A strike from nature, my death is secure
Saved from life by a power failure
My eye lets loose one final tear

Let Freedom Ring

Bombs bursting overhead
Dozens of soldiers lie here dead
On the ground, their blood runs red
Still, we move ahead

Targets hit, one by one
Enemy soldiers on the run
I pause to reload my gun
This battle will soon be won

A relentless attack is best
So onward we pressed
With no time for rest
I take a bullet in the chest

I cry out in pain
But its all in vain
The bomb blasts drive me insane
Finally the battle begins to wane

Under the pale light of the moon
The battlefield lies in ruin
Slowly dying, I need help soon
I hum a patriotic tune

As if on cue
A soldier comes to my rescue
So people get a clue
To our soldiers, our freedom is due

To them we owe everything
All the joys that freedom can bring
So everyone stand and sing
"Let freedom ring!"

Black Cloud

A ominous black cloud
Follows me around
No matter where I go
Its face it's sure to show
My life gets caught in a rut
Stinging like a paper cut
Through my life's strains
Black cloud just rains
Just when things go right
Black cloud comes into sight
Looming over my shoulder
Crashing down like a boulder
The storm in you is writhing
But I look to the bright horizon
Black cloud that follows me
Black cloud you let me be
Black cloud you have no power
Over me you will not tower

The On-Line Blues

Chatting on-line,
everything's fine.
Suddenly I hear
that word we all fear.
"Good-bye."
I sigh.
As sly as a fox
up pops a box.
"Internet connection lost."
For this, I pay a monthly cost??
I'm mad like a wild dervish.
They call this service.
My heads getting dizzy.
Now the connection service is busy.
I scream and wail!
I cant check my e-mail!
What can I do?
Maybe I'll sue.

I'll Be There

When your feeling blue
I'll be there next to you
If you're feeling sad
I'll be there to make you glad
If you're ever feeling down
I'll be there to cure that frown
If life leaves you feeling glum
I'll be there as your best chum
If you feel that none do care
I'll be there with love to share
If life makes you cry
I'll be there to wipe them dry
If you're feeling a loss or grief
I'll be there to turn over your new leaf
So if you're ever in despair
Remember...... I'll be there

The Meaning of Life

Life is stressful and full of tension
A search for serenity is my intention
The facts of life are very real
With them we all must deal
Everything in life has its cost
Without our friends we'd be lost
Life is full of ups and downs
Sometimes you smile, others you frown
Sometimes you laugh, others you cry
Life will have no meaning unless you try

Last Night

Last night I had a few beers
This morning my head is unclear
What I did, I am not sure
I visited bars, acted immature
I downed drink after drink
I soon lost all ability to think
The whole room was in a swirl
Dancing on tables, I did twirl
In my drunken condition
I lost all inhibition
So I grabbed a pretty girl
Groped her for a cheap thrill
I got a slap in the face
It was such a disgrace
So to save dignity and respect
I did something stupid, as you'd expect
I challenged a bouncer to a fight
It landed me in jail for the night
That's why in this cell, I did wake
Head pounding, regretting my mistake
I think there's a moral to this
But I was drunk , the moral I did miss

The Disgruntled Poet

I am the disgruntled poet
My words will clearly show it
For the wrath of the critic I have felt
It's not a feeling with which I have dealt
His harsh words left me for dead
These are the words that he said
"This poetry crap is for the birds
It's just a bunch of rhyming words
You only need half a brain
Don't even need to strain
You have no sense of humor
You must have a brain tumor"
Upon his review, I did depend
He hated me, my career's at an end
On this book I worked hard
I'm ruined by that tub of lard
If I could get a hold you now,
And I will someday, somehow
You will feel my wrath and anger
You Mr. Critic, are in danger
You might as well run for the border
I won't be stopped by a court order
For I am the disgruntled poet
And soon you will know it

If God Was Here Now

If God was here now,
what would he say
about the state of his world?
Would he look down with pride
at the wonders we've done?
Would he cry in despair
at the wars that we fight?
Would he show his face proudly
or hide in fear, for we killed his son?
If God was here now, what would you say?
These questions I ask you to ponder,
for I have a story to tell.
It will make you wonder.
The bible says that God will return.
He will judge and decide are fate.
Has he been here and already cast our fate?
Has he seen how we hate?
We murder and rape the innocent ones.
We wage wars in God's holy name.
Remember the holy crusades?
On this issue God is clear.
THOU SHALL NOT KILL!
We kill the living , we kill the unborn.
We alter our bodies from God's ideal view.
We lift up our faces, we alter our breasts,
we suction our tummies,
we poke holes in our bodies.

We paint under our skin.
We hide our true selves under these masks.
All because we don't like what God gave us.
Our God given beauty is all that we hide.
We like not what God gave us,
so we fixed it ourselves.
If God was here now,
would he see a future for us?
Our children are born innocent
but grow up to betray us.
Each generation that passes grows worse and worse.
Kids kill kids over the almighty dollar.
We mock God's name by pasting it on our money.
Our churches are now corporate
and live just for money.
Remember dear Jesus when he saw the church.
He was disgraced and tossed tables asunder.
Yet, still I am left to wonder.
Why are our churches still the same?
Our church is a business
fueled by greed and the dollar.
Our priest drives a Cadillac while a mother of four
walks over a mile to give her last dollar,
just to aide the church she believes in.
If God was here now,
 would he come out and say it
or would he just observe and judge us?

After all,
his dear son Jesus gave us our warning.
Is it too late? Has God decided our fate?
If I was to tell you God is here now
would you believe me or just laugh in my face?
If a secret I did tell you, how would you respond?
If I tell you that I am God,
what would you say to me?
Am I crazy? Would you lock me up
and throw me in a padded cell?
Or would you ignore me and go on your way?
Would you pick up and follow my way?
Am I serious or just delirious?
Well that's for you to decide.
God gave us the gift of free will.
God does not decide if we go to heaven or hell.
We choose our own fate
by the way we live each day.
If I was God and walked the earth today,
What do you think I would say?
Should the world stay or shall it move on
or has our sentence already been passed?
Have we been doomed to die at our own hands?
Think about it. You might be ashamed.
May God have mercy on us all!!!
Amen!!!

Claire L. Strough
Amherst, New York

My Mother My Best Friend is written in memory of
my mother Dorothy C. Hastings (1942-1974).
The Holy Child was the first poem
I ever wrote back in the ninth grade.
What Is A Sister is dedicated to my sister Dawn.

My Mother, My Best Friend
The Holy Child
You Are My Reason
What Is A Sister
You Are My One

My Mother, My Best Friend

There will never be another,
to take the place of my dear mother.
For I loved her so,
I don't know why she had to go.
Years have come, years have gone
but the pain goes on,
since the loss of my mother, my best friend.
God took her from me so quickly,
there was no chance to say good bye.
I still think of her in silence,
no one to see me cry.
She's gone from my eyes
so I can not see her,
but in my heart she will always be
my mother, my best friend.
Before I close my eyes,
I look up to the skies,
before me an image appears.
It is then that I know she's not so far,
for God has sent me an angel.
She's, my mother, my best friend.
On a picture woven in gold
I now and then see her face.
This is the picture I hold tenderly,
to love, cherish and never forget.
For, she was my mother, my best friend.

The Holy Child

Oh holy child, infant of joy,
Oh holy child, blessed baby boy.
Unto the virgin mother he was born,
the son of God in human form.

In a stable, he laid,
on a bed made of hay.
The stars shined so bright,
as angels watched through the night.

Three wise men came from afar.
Their compass and guidance was the Bethlehem star.
They came to worship the new born king,
while angels' voices echoed the joy as they sang.

Truly was he the new born king,
for all the world he brings.
No more shall sin and evil infest the earth,
for, all those who believe, he brings rebirth.

You Are My Reason

You are my reason,
for waking up each morning
and starting a fresh new day.
For the air that I breath,
which keeps me here to stay.
You are my reason,
for seeing the ocean once again
and hearing the tides roll in.
Because of you, I feel the hot rays
of the sun upon my chin.
You are my reason,
that I feel so much desire
My, soul has been set on fire.
This wonderful love of yours,
keeps me going on living.
You are my reason,
for laughing when I feel like crying.
For giving me the will
that makes me go on trying
when, I feel like giving up.
You are my reason,
I fell in love with you
and it will always be true.
Until, death do us part,
you'll remain in my heart.

You Are My One

We met in a special place,
that I can never replace.
It's taken up a lot of empty space,
that's given us a special grace

As I gaze into your eyes,
its as if I'm staring at the bright blue sky.
Yet, not to say I love you, for I am shy
please, never ask me why.

As I look into your face,
all I feel is your sweet embrace.
No man has ever put me in such a place
but you have filled that empty space.

Through suffering, I've opened the door
to something I never felt before.
My heart cries out for more
Its you, whom I adore.

I'm not sure why my feelings are so strong
for my love has always been wrong.
Could it be, I've yearned for so long
that a love like yours could be so strong?

For each day I given thanks for this love we share
I see it in fields and flowers, everywhere.
You have made a difference, knowing you care
and that you will always be there.

You are my dream come true,
you have taken away my blues.
My days are empty without you,
I need you here each day through.

You have made my eyes see
that no one else awaits for me.
My heart is, where it wants to be
Your love has set me free.

What Is A Sister

A sister is someone who is always there,
not even the distance can keep them apart.
The wonderful memories we hold in our heart.
A sister is someone whom you trust
more then anyone else in the world.
A sister is there to talk about anything:
she is there to listen to you.
A sister is there during happy times
and shed tears with during sad.
A sister is there to make you laugh
when you feel like crying.
A sister will help you pick up the pieces
when your life is falling apart.
A sister is someone to be proud of
for all that she has become.
A sister is your best friend.
Sister, you are everything to me,
you are my sister, my best friend.

Ann Marie McMahon
10/16/1974
Buffalo, New York

LYA....

Untitled
LEAVES
Insanity
No Future?
Weak

Untitled

Here I am at dusk lying in a blanket of sand. Here in the cold, damp weather. I feel a heat, a passion beneath my skin, sinking all the way to my soul. A craving for life. I want to learn every aspect of humanity, and even beyond that. I want to feel every emotion. I want to taste the inner soul of every last thing that touches the earth. And only you, my teacher, can give this gift to me. Only you can hear my cry for peace. A peace within myself for that I desire. Thrill me dear teacher, so I can lay here on the beach and praise you. Discover me, for I need to be heard. Help me, so we both can be satisfied. The feelings I feel are real, and need to be understood. And only you, my teacher, can give this gift to me.

LEAVES

THE TREES
SO PLEASANT, SO QUIET.
THE GRASS
SO RIGID, SO TALL.
THE LEAVES-
THEY JUST LAY THERE.

THE BIRDS
SO BRAVE, SO STRONG.
THE CLOUDS
SO WHITE, SO PURE.
THE LEAVES-
THEY JUST LAY THERE.

THE FLOWERS
SO FIRM, SO COLORFUL.
THE SOIL
SO MOIST, SO BLACK.
THE LEAVES-
THEY JUST LAY THERE.

THE WAR
SO DEEP, SO SAD.
THE BLOOD
SO RED, SO MEANINGFUL.
THE SOLDIERS-
THEY JUST LAY THERE.

Insanity

I gaze at the moon upon me
I inhale the air around me
I touch the grass of despair
Wishing my heart was there
I stop and sit on the earth's natural floor
The dew covers me as I scream for more
Mother nature tucks me in
The night surrounds my secret sin
Only creatures sleep near me
Here underneath this dead tree
The rain is making me crazy
Truth is here and it doesn't phase me
I cannot keep hiding here in shame
It is slowly driving me insane.

No Future?

She knelt in the middle of the room,
Screaming on her knees.
Don't leave me, please!
As she reached at his sleeve.
The door closed,
But she had to believe,
He'll be back, I know.
He'll be back, God PLEASE!

What future do I have?
He is gone, and I'm alone.
She thought all day and night,
Then she reached for the phone.
She dialed anyone she knew,
Anyone who was home.
Someone help me please,
He is all that I have known.

Then she called me up
As if God intervened
She explained it all,
Every word she had screamed.
I asked her if she loved him,
Even though he was so mean.
She proclaimed her love
And all her hopes and dreams.
I said why do you love him
And a light finally beamed…

I thought he was my future
I never thought of letting go?
She starting thinking,
Say it isn't so?
All these years I was forgetting,
All these years I didn't know.
I could just be myself,
And have a future for my own.

Weak

You said that I was weak,
But you've never seen me strong.
You said I was not pretty,
But you never really looked.
You said I wasn't smart,
But you never tickled my mind.
You said I would never be a writer,
But I have never stopped writing.
You said I wasn't funny,
But you didn't get the joke.
You said I would never make it,
But I am doing well.
You said I was weak,
But you've never seen me strong.

Jennifer L. Olague Balkus
October 20, 1970
Ontario, California

My Grandfather was written in memory of my
grandfather Leonard Stephen Chilton (1912-1984)
Wake Up was a poem written about the love of my
souls' homeland…Oahu.
The End? A poem written about lost love.
Her was written for my sis and BEST friend.
Knowing written about the spirits of loved ones
who have passed on but are always with me

My Grandfather
Wake Up
The End?
Her
Knowing
Copyright 2003 Jennifer L. Olague Balkus

My Grandfather

He collected stamps
And smoked cigarettes
Eyed precious coins
And gambled on stallions
Loved lemon drops and Coors
Investigated fingerprints
And worked with steel
He drove a Chevy
And wore thin glasses
This man was handsome
With a killer smile
And was larger than life
He cheated at Chinese Checkers
And was a whiz at Solitaire
He gave solid hugs
And mended all our wounds
Tenderness and warmth
Were always felt with him
He was thin and pale
But always strong
Intelligent and witty
How I miss him so
His name means "Brave or Strong as the lion"
And "A crown or Garland"
If there's nothing we have left
Don't let his memory die too.

Wake Up

As the sun goes down it pulls at my heart
The grass is fresh and green ready to slumber
Colored leaves scattered across the earth
Their destination is unknown
Yet they will be happy when they arrive
Wind wrestles the almost bare trees
And caresses my skin
Daylight is falling asleep now
I look to the sky in amazement
So clear you can touch the stars
Faceless people with their heads bent down
Wondering through the crowded streets
Stop what you are doing
Pause for just one second
And look at our beautiful land
Look at what God has blessed us with
Don't let it all fade away

The End?

In slumber my thoughts race
And my heart aches for you
My pulse beating wildly
Makes me feel like a child again
My once illusive dreams you made erotic
For months we've been lovers
In ecstasy I call out your name
You caressing my heart, my very soul
Hearing your voice is such sweet agony
In my mind our conversations roam
The good, the bad…I just don't understand
I shouldn't be surprised this happened
I knew it would come to an end
But never imagined it would be this way
You don't want to talk to me anymore
You won't look at me
Those eyes once so filled with love
Are so guarded…so distant
Our hearts will never meet again?
Will our lips never touch?
Illusions shattered,
Dreams forgotten,
Promises…broken
Tears, confusion and heartache
Is this how our love will end?
Babee, please tell me that you didn't say "Goodbye"

Her

I'm in an emotional whirlwind
I need to see her beautiful face
To hear her caring voice
The way her eyes caress everything she looks at
The smell of her skin
The touch of her hand...
Leave me breathless
She calms me
I crave the serenity she brings to my life
I love her more than even I thought was possible
She anchors all my fears
And gives me hope
When the last of mine has faded
If I could wish for anything in the universe
I would wish for her happiness
Just to see her smile...
I would do anything
It is because of her
That I am a better person

Knowing

Knowing you are there I feel so alone
I can feel your presence and then it's gone
Who are you?
I want...
No, I have to know
So much a part of my thoughts
In my minds eye your smiles,
Your voices cradle me
Wiping away every pain
Imagined or real
Memories seared into my soul...
Will my memories be enough?
In a trance I methodically function
Trying to "be" without you
You are the pieces my heart has been yearning for
A lifetime ago I seem to have loved you
Knowing you are there

Printed in the United States
48418LVS00002B/4